POWER SOURCE

Living a Life of Lasting Joy

Monica Lewis

Table of Contents

FOREWORD

Power Source, is a wide-open window into the soul of author Monica Lewis. When Monica and I first met, I knew we were kindred spirits. She possessed a calm, easy-going spirit and effortlessly radiated positivity and optimism, especially when facing situations where I personally lacked such grace. We were instant friends because we balanced each other in a way that was truly divine. Her story provides insight on how she can stand and smile optimistically in the face of any challenge that comes her way. She has transformed her own health, relationships, financial and spiritual life using her own power source.

This inspirational story provides an up-close look at the devastating heart break that led Monica to discover her Power Source, to rise above her circumstances and transform her life from one of defeat to one of victory. Monica is a passionate and brilliantly effective transformational coach because of her unique journey and her ability to empathize. She blends her business acumen with personal life lessons, to masterfully help people create the change they desire in any area of their personal lives and businesses.

This book is a must-read. It outlines simple steps that anyone who feels stuck in any area of life can take, to move from a place of brokenness to a place of true joy through the Power Source Challenge. Monica's transparency and willingness to share her darkest moments, inspires readers to discover their own renewable Power Source.

- *Dr. Kivette Parkes*

Naturopathic Physician at The Lifestyle Clinic and Founder of Not Just Weight

INTRODUCTION

Do you know that within you, there is power? Within you, there is strength and an internal knowing that is so much greater than anything you have experienced before. No matter how high or how low your life may feel at this moment, there is a power within you that can create a life of limitless possibilities. When you become aware of spirit, you realize that God is the author of everything and you can tap into the Power Source that is within you. The strength is in everyone. The difference lies in whether you learn to access that strength or whether you allow it to simply lay dormant, waiting for you to tap into your fountain. The choice is yours.

In the next few pages, I will share with you how I discovered my Power Source and was able to plug in, access, and activate the tools that helped me break down all the barriers in my life to live the life of limitless joy I now possess. The Power Source Challenge will allow you to confront your fears, unmask your insecurities, and ascend to a dimension of personal freedom you never thought possible. Your Power Source is waiting...

NO IDEA OF SUCCESS

At the moment you are reading these words, I feel so blessed to have a beautiful three-year-old daughter and a wonderfully supportive boyfriend. I am grateful to have helpful and supportive people in my life—my friends and my family and I'm thankful to have done exceptionally well in business.

As a successful entrepreneur of multiple businesses, I not only own a business currently, but I also sold a mental health business in 2015. My partners and I made some great money with that sale. More than that, I vividly remember the day we sold the clinic. I was sitting at that conference table feeling my breath moving at a heightened pace. I was excited while simultaneously feeling nervous, and somewhat in disbelief. I knew that I was about to do something that I could only classify as a miracle to me. It was an anomaly, something that was not supposed to happen for me. How could I, a young black woman, sit across from older, distinguished, white businessmen and discuss the possibility of them purchasing my company for an extraordinary amount of money. In that very moment, I knew, without hesitation that all things were possible. However, that belief was not always the case.

Growing up, I lived in an impoverished neighborhood in Charlotte, North Carolina. My inner foundation was weakened with the struggles and obstacles around me. My stepdad loved our family but struggled with the pressures of life, responsibilities, and the expectations of being a minister's son in a locally well-known family. He found his outlet in drugs and partying. Sadly, his escape became his addiction.

My mom did everything she could to stand in the gap his absence left. She tried to be the financial and emotional support for the family when he could not. Mom was very structured and managed to meet our physical needs, but often the guidance and support we needed emotionally was not there. Most days, she lived in a state of mental suffering and angst from worrying, hurt and betrayal. Those emotions took up so much room in her life, there was very little left to give us. The void left me wanting to get away and escape the chaos at home. I cried out to others for the attention and affection every child needs and I spent most of my time with friends and people out in the streets.

Without realizing it, I was developing a thought pattern of inadequacy and an expectation of insufficiency both emotionally and physically. Deep down in the fiber of my being, I developed a pattern of belief that life was designed to be a struggle. I had a low trust threshold for people. I constantly felt that the comforts and joys of life were always fleeting. Comfort and joy would be present one moment but gone the next. I was aware they existed, but I could not find them within my reach. The expectation life created for me was that it should be hard. I, constantly, lived with the notion that a life of lasting joy was not possible, that it was only a fairy tale. Though I may have desired the life I saw in the movies, it would never manifest in my reality.

For the most part, everyone around me lived and breathed the same belief system. The refrigerator would be full when my mom got paid, but for several days before her next check, she struggled to pull a meal together. Some days she would be happy to see us and would spend quality time with us. She would show interest in our school work, what we liked, disliked, and what we were thinking. However, most days she was cold, distant, and angry. Deep down, we knew it was because life was so difficult for her and she was trying to process it the best way she knew how. That knowledge didn't negate the responsibility of raising fully mentally, physically, and spiritually sound children. Thus mom's difficulties became our difficulties.

A PRAYER OF FRUSTRATION

As I grew older, my view of myself and life didn't alter very much. The experience of college helped to build my confidence in some areas but made it worse in others. I always knew I was intelligent and could make great grades when I applied myself. I knew that I had a very small but solid and trusted group of friends who would be there when I needed them. There were also some family members who tried to be there for me, and there were others who I, absolutely, could not count on.

What I had not come to realize, though, was the quality and depth of my self-worth. What I did not know was how to be treated by a man nor did I know how I should treat him. What I did not know was that I deserved and could achieve continual happiness. Ultimately, what I did not know was that God was there for me, rooting for me, and walking with me. In my mind, the God I knew from my childhood did more judging and punishing than loving. These were the sum of my truths, this was the foundation of my belief, and these were the lenses from which I viewed the world.

In my late twenties, I met a man who was smart, outgoing and just fun to be around. We both worked at the Department of Juvenile Justice and had a passion for helping kids who came from backgrounds like ours. He, like I, grew up without a biological father in the home and was determined that he was going to be different than his father. He had two small kids from a previous marriage and wanted to be a great father to them. He also had a desire to be a parental figure for the young men who did not have a male role model around.

I really admired those qualities about him.

Within a few days of meeting, he communicated that he had an attraction for me. I brushed it off, of course. I just thought he was asking me out because I was the new office conquest. A few men had already tried and failed and I refused to be a part of the office chatter or gossip. There was enough of that going on …if you know what I mean. Eventually, though, I gave in and agreed to go on a date with him. Fast forward, in 2004, we were married.

One night after celebrating our one year anniversary, I found myself lying in bed anxiously tossing back and forth. It was three o'clock in the morning. Unable to sleep, I got up to check on our kids. I peeked into each room and briefly watched them sleep. I always found it intoxicating to watch them at peace, but when I headed back to my room, I couldn't escape the feelings of dread that continued to wash over me.

The reality of my situation plagued me night after night. I was haunted by feelings of betrayal, loneliness, and anger. I should have been lying, cuddled up next to my husband of one year. Instead, I was alone, wondering whether he was in the arms of another woman. In my heart, I knew that's exactly where he was, but he would never admit to it. In fact, he continued to look me in the eye and lie to my face. Over and over he would say to me, "I would never choose another woman over you." He was adamant that I was the one with the problem; the one who was making things up, the one with the issues, the one who was crazy.

So, there I was, once again. Shallow breath. In bed. Alone. With my mind frantic, staring up at the ceiling, and wondered how could he do this to me! I did not deserve this. I began crying uncontrollably, somehow feeling responsible for my situation. I chose him to partner with me in this thing called life, yet he didn't love me, he didn't respect me, and all I could think about was why. Why couldn't I make him love me the way I needed to be loved? Why wasn't I pretty enough, sexy enough, or smart enough? Why wasn't I just ENOUGH? With no answers, I began to beg God to change me, to give me the right things to say to keep my husband at home. I begged Him to show me what to wear so he would choose me. I begged Him to give me the strength to endure. The more I begged, though, the angrier I became.

I called my husband's cell phone twice, but there was no answer. The third time I called, a woman answered the phone. I couldn't believe it. Every shred of dignity I had, left me at that moment. Swallowing my pride, I begged this woman to speak to *my* husband.   Not like a wife, but like a customer waiting for a representative to resolve my issue, I was put on hold. I was shocked and in a state of disbelief. I felt like I was going to die.   My mind was racing, yet I couldn't stifle my curiosity.   Who was she? What did she look like? Why did he keep choosing her over me?   Then, the line went dead.

The tiny bit of sanity that was left was gone with the click of the phone disconnection. Disgusted, I threw it across the room and spewed words of hatred at the only person I felt was responsible...GOD!

"God, how could you do this to me! I deserve better than this! I have been good to this man! I stay here night after night taking care of his children; helping them with their homework, cooking for them, and making sure they are taken care of while he repeatedly has sex with

other women. He doesn't even have the decency to tell me the truth; that he just doesn't love me! Instead, he lies and makes me feel like I am crazy. God, please give me the proof that I need to move on from this! Help me to know whether I should stay or move on in peace," I cried.

At that moment, the door opened and my son came in the room. He heard me moving around the house and he was concerned. When he saw the tears running down my face, he reached out to hug me. The closeness of our relationship was a blessing, a blessing that most couldn't understand. Sometimes I did not even understand it. I was happy that both of my husband's children loved me the way they did. Not being the children's biological parent did not matter in that moment. The instant hurt I saw in his eyes seeing me crying let me know that it was not biology that was important. He just wanted to take my tears away. Trying to cover my pain, I kissed his forehead and sent him back to bed. Despite the way their father treated me, I wanted to protect them and their innocence. They didn't deserve this any more than I.

At 7 a.m. the next morning, I awoke on the floor where I'd cried and prayed myself to sleep. After my emotional rantings to God, I was so tired that I never even made it to the bed. I was stirred awake by the sound of someone moving around in the kitchen. Thinking it was one of the children, I entered to find my husband making something to eat as if nothing was wrong...as if he hadn't just been out the entire night.

When I walked into the room, he greeted me with a simple, *"Hello."* In my head, I was yelling, *"Are you serious? Hello! That's all you have to say to me!"* But the kids were sitting at the table, so I mustered up a very low and squeaky,

"Hello," in return. As calmly as I could, I continued, *"Where were you last night?"*

"You know where I was. Where do I always go on Friday nights? You act as if this is a new thing. I was with the boys. I always go out with the boys on Friday nights to watch the local football games," he said. *"I didn't realize there were local football games that lasted all night. I, also, didn't know that women attended those games with you and your friends,"* I replied.

"What do you mean, women?"
"Like the woman who answered your phone after 3 a.m. last night."
"Girl, you are crazy. That was my friend's cousin. She must have heard my phone ringing and answered it."
"Well, you never came to the phone."
"Because I knew you'd be trippin'. In fact, I could have gotten home a few hours ago, but I decided to sleep in the parking lot at the grocery store up the

street because I wanted to get some rest before I got home. I wasn't in the mood to hear your mouth and those lies you make up in your head."

Anger welled up inside me again, and tears streamed down my face. Unable to control my emotions, I ran out of the room so I wouldn't frighten the children.

I managed to pull myself together to help the kids get dressed. We had a full day of visiting family and friends, so I stifled my feelings so I could get through the day. The whole time, I felt like a fraud because our family had so many divisive secrets. We were simply living a lie. It wasn't long afterward I learned that there was no freedom in living a lie. God could not bless who we pretended to be.

Before leaving the house, I checked the mail. In it, I discovered my husband's monthly credit card statement. It had never come to the house before, yet there it was. I decide to run back into the house to open it. I slipped into the closet out of eye sight. I was shaking nervously because somehow, I knew what I would find.

Viewing the statement, I noticed several purchases for hotel stays in a neighboring city. I knew I had not stayed in those places with him. My heart was broken, but I was thankful that I finally had the proof I needed to call him on his lies. I wondered if this was God answering my prayers, but because I lacked confidence, I quickly dismissed it as a coincidence. Suddenly, I heard him call my name. *"Monica, let's go. My mom is expecting us."* I swallowed my pride, put the envelope in the top of my closet under a stack of jeans, and walked to the car.

On our way to visit his mom, we stopped at a gas station. Both he and one of the children were in a hurry to use the restroom. As he was unstrapping his son from the seat, he shoved his phone at me and asked me to hold it until he returned. I was instantly annoyed, but I didn't know that it was soon about to be a blessing in disguise. Glancing at the phone, I could not ignore the strong desire to flip through its contents.

To my surprise, he had not taken the time to lock the screen. Coincidence #2? As I scrolled the call log, the number in the last called list showed up in his phone as 70437625416485. This was odd because phone numbers only have ten digits. Then it hit me. The last four digits were the code to his voicemail! I was speechless! It couldn't actually be this easy.

Frantically, I committed the numbers to memory before he returned. This had to be God's miraculous answer to my prayers. I had asked for proof in my time of need, and He answered my prayer. This time I knew it was not a coincidence. God was showing His love. I asked, and the proof was given.

This experience birthed a new interesting inner knowing in my life. It was empowering, but not in a way I thought it might be. I began to think to myself that if God came to me in that space, as low as I was, and with as much misperception I had in my mind of God, of love, and of myself, what did that mean? God must love me. This began my personal journey—my interchange with God.

THE BEGINNING OF MY JOURNEY

I wish I could tell you that I woke up one morning completely brand new. However, that wasn't the case. Things didn't change overnight. It was a development over time. Gradually, I developed new ways of thinking. My personal development consisted of accumulating tools to catapult me to a woman filled with purpose and action; a woman sure of herself. That experience in my past has helped me live, now, as a strong, powerful, and self-assured woman capable of accomplishing things that, at that time, I didn't even think were possible.

When I started my journey, I was making less than $38,000 annually. Less than ten years later, I was consulting for multimillion dollar companies and I owned several successful Mental Health

Clinics. My business partners and I sold several of the Mental Health Clinics for seven figures. It was a massive shift from the woman who didn't think she was enough and barely got by, to the strong, powerful woman I am today.

Right now, I can tell you that I feel blessed every day. Through the course of my journey, I began living differently. I learned that if I had the right source, I had strength. The right Power Source was like a pillar in my life; something that helped me in both the high and the low times of my life to move forward. I learned firsthand that I could change my perspective. I know that all things are possible, now, because of the Power Source I tapped into within me.

Your power will show up in your life in various ways. For me, it meant being able to break old patterns. I began to see how God saw me and through that, I was able to see differently. When I began to see differently, I was able to help others who felt they weren't enough. It gave me the ability to love others in a way that I really hadn't understood or known before. More importantly, it gave me the capacity to practice radical forgiveness. I possessed the ability to constantly forgive people for the wrongs that they knowingly or unknowingly perpetrated against me. Instead of looking at the one instance of hurt I was experiencing, I began to look at the bigger picture for the person causing the pain. In most cases, the pain reflects a deeper hurt that has not healed, and now a dysfunctional habit of action has developed to ease the pain from the deeply rooted hurt. The perpetrator can no longer see who they are hurting, all they can see in that instant is the weight of their own pain, and they act accordingly.

I cannot begin to share how freeing this wisdom and action has been in my life.

This has allowed me to love freely and to create space for true love; love built on abundance, freedom, and trust and not one based on control and deceit allowing people to be who they truly are, forgiving them when causing harm. Now, instead of holding grudges or exacting revenge, I can release the feelings and the people responsible for the hurt. This process empowered me to break the shackles of victimization and release the pain of the hurt further along with me in life, in some cases, putting an end to the cycle of pain.

By now, you may be asking yourself, *"How can I do this, too?"* Like me, you've probably gone around looking for love in everything and everyone outside of yourself. The place to start is loving yourself first. Everything in your life that does not align with pure love is something that's not of God. Any thoughts that you have that are not based in love are doing you a disservice.

They're continuing to encourage you to live in fear; to make you feel that you are not enough, to always tell you what you can't do, and to judge, criticize, and condemn you. Those are the thoughts that you should examine. Finding a different source of power will help you learn to tap into that inner knowing that God has placed inside all of us. Love and fear cannot exist together. The more you train yourself to replace fear with love, the less room there will be for your negative thoughts.

I invite you to take my Power Source Challenge. I know it can change your life. It can change how and where you see God. I developed it from the experience I had that night when I learned how to have a clear conversation with God. Over the course of time, even though at first, I didn't know what I was doing, I began to see what was working in my life. I have created a program so that you, too, can tap into your power source. The steps are not complicated, but like all re-training, it requires consistent practice.

Every night before you go to bed, list 3-5 positive things from your day. Start off with the first positive thought that comes to mind. It doesn't have to be anything big. It can be that you got a kind word or a kind note from someone. Write each positive thought down. When you awake the next day, read the good things from the day before. Go through each of the 3-5 things that happened the day prior, and thank God for them. For example, if you got a loving note from your brother, thank God for providing it. Say, *"Thank you, God, for loving me enough to provide me this loving note today."* Go through each item and end by saying, *"Thank you God, for loving me enough to do all these things for me yesterday."* This will set your intentions for the day.

Whether you realize it or not, doing this will start forming a habit that creates a shift in your thought pattern. It will enable you to show up differently in your life and the world. As you practice this challenge over time, you will tap into your power source. Gratitude is the single most powerful tool to reframe your brain and reframe your unconscious knowing.

JOY CONSCIOUSNESS VERSUS DIS-EASE CONSCIOUSNESS

After some time practicing the challenge, I noticed that there were days when I could hear God more clearly than others. These were the days when I experienced the benefits and guidance of my relationship stronger than others. What was the factor that changed when I felt out of step or disconnected from my Power source? After closer examination, I realized the answer. The days I was consistent with doing the challenge and was more in tune with His presence, were the days that blessings and contentment seemed to flow. On those days, I found myself caught up in worry and anxiety about life, I noticed that I could not hear Him or feel the strength and guidance of our relationship. By this time, I had been in a close relationship with God long enough to know that even if I didn't feel Him, He was still there. Yet, when I was filled with fear, anxiety and worry, it was as if a thick fog was present allowing me no access to Him. When in that state of desperation, I felt separated from God and alone. When in that space, I was less forgiving of myself and more often hurtful towards others. I realized that there was a pattern emerging. I had two distinct ways of being, two distinct patterns of thought. One, I now label as Joy Consciousness and the other Dis-ease Consciousness.

I knew that I wanted to understand these concepts on a deeper level. I wanted to study how this new relationship could impact my life. I wanted to feel God's presence all the time as it did not feel good when I felt alone, when I lashed out at others, or felt anxiety, jealousy, or hatred. That was not how I wanted to live my life. I wanted to live life in a state of perpetual love, joy, and compassion for others. Therefore, I purposed a journey to learn more about these feelings. Was there truly a way I could purposefully tap into joy more often?

What I learned from personal experience and research was that there is an internal voice of wellness we each possess. Some call it intuition. Some call it the Holy Spirit. Some call it nature.

This wellness or Power Source is directly connected to God. With it, you have the privilege of tapping into God's eternal wisdom. Your unique blueprint of wellness is designed to guide you to your purpose and help you achieve lasting joy and happiness.

Joy Consciousness is what you feel when you are at peace. You experience a sense of contentment as if life is rigged in your favor. All is well. Joy Consciousness does not mean you must be in a state of elation at all times. There are various emotions that you can feel when you receive energy from Joy Consciousness.

Dis-ease Consciousness is when you feel angst, or feel like something is not right in your mind and body. In this place, you are not at peace. You feel as if you are alone. You feel like you are not enough. You do not feel worthy or loved. You do not have support. You are afraid of a potential outcome. You feel like others are out to get you. You feel that you will never have enough money for your needs because there simply is not enough to go around. You feel like you have to get yours first, or someone will take it from you, or that you are going to lose something important to you at any moment. You feel under attack, but without a real present danger. You feel like the weight of the world rests on your shoulders. These feelings are what I call LIES, but they can completely dominate your thoughts. Deep in your subconscious you know they are lies but you feel powerless to do anything about them. If I asked you at this moment, if there are any lies holding you back from achieving your blessings, I know you could immediately write down several. Isn't that amazing? That is the eternal power source within you telling you that you are meant to love more, have more, and enjoy more. Instead, we choose, over and over again, to believe the lies. We have become trained to believe the imposter in our heads. Take heart, my friends, if you can train yourself to believe the lies, you can re-train yourself to believe the truth!

The emotions you feel are a direct reflection of the thought that you chose at that moment. In other words, your emotions serve as a gauge and are a reflection of the quality of thoughts you are thinking. If you are feeling dis-ease, there is a LIE, or an imposter as I like to call it, somewhere in the midst!

Joy Consciousness	Dis-ease Consciousness
Love	Fear
Peace	Worry
Hope	Anxiety
Appreciation	Worry
Ecstasy	Blame
Freedom	Hate
Positivity	Jealousy
Passion	Guilt
Excitement	Unworthiness
Elation	Insecurity
Contentment	Grief
Enthusiasm	Powerlessness
Happiness	Hopelessness
Eagerness	Shame
Kindness	Overwhelm
Delight	Pessimism

When dis-ease thoughts dominate your consciousness, you live in a perpetual place of unhappiness. You have fleeting moments of joy, but the weight of the dis-ease will not allow long lasting joy to flow. Most people are living their lives wallowing in dis-ease.

The most beautiful thing God revealed to me is how to purposely move back to Joy Consciousness. Whenever I feel dis-ease in my body and emotions, I know that I am thinking a thought that does not serve me. I am thinking a lie! So, I begin to examine those thoughts. I examine how true they are. In most situations, I found I am feeling angst because of something that is not concrete. The thought has no real merit. It is something that is rooted in the future or the past, but I am choosing to live life in the present, in the here and now.

Examples of the Lies we tell ourselves:

I will never make the money that I want to make in this industry.

Men all cheat at one point or another, those who say they don't just have never been caught.

All rich people make their money by stepping on other people to get it.

There is something wrong with me!

Nothing good ever happens to me.

The only reason they have love and abundance is because they are lucky.

Whenever I want to break this cycle of dis-ease thinking, I practice gratitude. Gratitude will break the cycle of dis-ease and move me back into a state of joy.

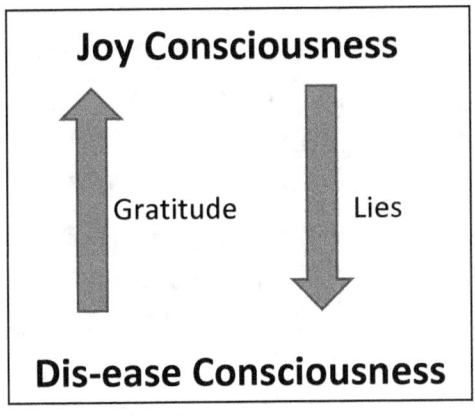

Purposely utilizing gratitude is not only an important life skill to learn and master, it's also an extremely important aspect of consistently attracting to yourself the joy and abundance that we all desire, aspire toward, and without exception deserve to experience in life.

It is a thought muscle that you will want to constantly strengthen! Make a conscious choice to look for the blessing in everything in life. Even when you are at your worst times, there is something that you can be grateful for.

Looking back on my marriage, I know that the entire experience was a blessing. One of my lowest points in life caused me to expand and receive the greatest joy in my life. I could have chosen to resent him or to stay in a state of mistrust. My thought patterns could have still been rooted in betrayal and insecurity, but I CHOSE something different. I chose to forgive him, to love others, to expect more, to move on purpose, and trust in possibilities. That choice freed me. That choice paved the way to a closer relationship with God. That choice caused me to get wealth and that choice brought me a new reciprocal type of intimate love. I choose daily to live in gratitude.

BE PURPOSEFUL (PURPOSE-FILLED) IN UNLEASHING THE POWER WITHIN YOU!!

The two areas we have examined will lead to significant change and inner growth. With those two concepts settled in your mind and heart, let's expand our re-training to six solid pillars that will lead to a complete transformation in your life and thought processes. We are about to learn how to develop a daily practice that will allow access to Power Source.

Know that we don't seek perfection here. The gifts are developed in the journey. One day builds on the day before, moving you ever closer to Joy Consciousness.

1) The Power of Knowing You Are Enough

We were each created as unique beings. Inside you exists a blueprint to your goals, dreams, wants, and desires. You have within you a way to access every decision. It can be based on knowing that in every decision you have made, you did the best you could with what you knew at that moment. This will help you be in peace in your own personal journey and allow you to take ownership over the highs and lows of your life. This sounds great, doesn't it?

The key is to "apply" it. That's where the challenge comes in! This can be a perplexing step. We love to beat ourselves up for our past. We love to beat others up for what they have done wrong. People who are hard on others are very critical of themselves. Acting in a constant spirt of Grace will allow more love in for yourself and others. Those of us who have worked with teens or have children from the early teens to even middle age know that children love to lament about how we have unjustly treated them in one way or another. Do you have the inner resolve to listen to their words, apologize, tell them you love them, and remind them you always acted in their best interest with the tools and the knowledge you had at that time. Remembering the time when you felt unheard as well? And then....LET IT GO! It's the practical application that can trip us up at this stage. For example, it's not the theory of letting go of our self-blame for losing our temper that will change our lives, it's the action, the actual doing that will change our lives. I can tell you from experience that every single time you honestly take this step, you emerge a little stronger in your core than you were before. You will emerge a little stronger in your feelings of self-worth. Every time you love yourself when you have done something wrong or you feel unworthy, you are allowing a space of healing within yourself and others. You are allowing the internal power source to speak with you more clearly.

Guilt, condemnation, and insecurity are the most powerful blockers to hearing that inner voice. Don't allow this to be the case! Be vigilant. I started with "You are Enough" for a reason. This is the cornerstone that supports all the other steps of growth.

2) The Power of Community

The people you associate with have a direct influence on the person you are now and who you are going to be. It is beneficial to learn how to attract people that inspire you to stretch to another level. These are the people who practice gratitude and the people who are motivating you to do more and be better; not the people that naturally drag you down. Seek to have purposeful people around you who support you emotionally. I call this your Intensive Care Unit (I.C.U). Your I.C.U will be there for you as you go through the ups and downs of life. They are there to help you feel connected, loved and supported. Your I.C.U is the circle of people that provide a safe space for you to be who you really are in your strength and in your vulnerability. These will be people who play an active role in helping you to live in Joy Consciousness. In fact, sharing the concepts in this book with your I.C.U will allow you and your inner circle to be in harmony with connection, love, and support. Can you imagine the people closest to you all purposefully living in Joy Consciousness? Take a moment to think of the impact that alone would make in your life.

You also want to purposefully have people around you that push you to reach your personal, financial, and career goals. I call this your Dream Team. Your Dream Team should be filled with the people who are already successful in the areas that you want to grow in. This is the group of people who hold you accountable to achieving goals and pursuing answers to the things in life that keep you up at night. These are the goals that really excite you. Being in close proximity to your Dream Team will allow you to model ways of thinking and concepts that are proven to work. These are people who have the knowledge and experience to push you out of your comfort zone. They help you see options that you may not be open to because of habituated ways of thinking. They challenge you, when you begin to believe the lies that hold you back from achieving success.

Be aware of the people you spend most of your time with. Analyze the last forty-eight hours of your life. Who did you spend the most time with? Do they fit in one or both of the categories described above? If the people in your life do not meet this criterion, you are likely to continue with the same mindset and habits you are in now with limited growth, including the thoughts and habits that do not serve you. You are a reflection of the people around you! So begin building your Intensive Care Unit and Dream Team today!

To really grow within your community, you'll have to ask for help. That probably sounds scary, but if they are the type of supportive people described above, they are probably there waiting to be asked. These are people who love to serve. Don't be afraid, reach out and ask for help.

3) The Power of Forgiveness

There is great freedom in forgiveness. Each day, take the time to forgive all those who have hurt you. When you forgive someone who has hurt you, the forgiveness actually blesses you. Forgiveness releases you from many of the lies that are rooted in dis-ease. You know the lies: that you are not loved, that you are alone and have no support, that you can't trust anyone, and that you are under attack. These are all thoughts that are usually attached to an experience where you have been injured and have chosen not to forgive. No one is perfect, myself included. I err against people I love all the time. I get angry. I say things that I may not mean to say. In fact, I almost always forget birthdays. In most cases my intentions are good. I do not get up in the morning thinking…. "hmmm, I would like to hurt my sister's feelings today" or how much it would make my day to make someone cry. In analyzing that for myself, I believe that most people have the best of intentions as well. This has allowed me to look beyond my hurt and give others the benefit of the doubt, look at the bigger picture, ask myself where is this hurt coming from, and then choose to continuously look at people through the lenses of compassion and grace. Most often when people are hurting you or someone else, the lies that spawn from a state of dis-ease consciousness are the driving force behind the hurtful action. The compulsion to hurt is coming from feeling separated from Power Source or wellness. We hurt and lash out because we feel anxiety, fear, and lack. This knowledge has freed me from the need to hold grudges and pushes me to forgive much quicker.

Now I practice radical forgiveness. When you are not in a place of forgiveness, you are literally the one drinking the poison of your own thoughts and blocking the doorway to lasting joy. We frequently think we can't or shouldn't forgive because the person who hurt us does not deserve forgiveness. Now don't get me wrong, forgiveness doesn't mean that you have to continuously set yourself up for an ongoing attack but allows a chance to open a clear emotional path. We believe that our lack of forgiveness hurts them. Sadly, the one held back is us. Serve yourself and set yourself free to experience the power found in forgiveness.

4) The Power of Breaking Negative Self-Talk

When you hear your own negative chatter, you have to discern whether the thoughts are going to move you closer to your goals and closer to a state of Joy. In every conversation and every thought, create a pattern of asking yourself, "Does this serve me or does it work against me?" "Is this thought true, or am I choosing to believe a lie?" I now realize that when I take action from a place of fear, anxiety or control of others, I end up blocking my blessings.

But when I take action from a place of joy, inspiration, and intuition I am moving in conjunction with all-knowing, limitless power and wisdom.

Growing your gratitude muscle and using positive affirmations, will retrain your thoughts and your mind to start having a self-dialogue that empowers you and helps you each day to tap into your Power Source. Rather than beat yourself up., remember that you did the best you could with what you knew at the time.

5) The Power of Giving

Giving is a strong and powerful act as is in the power of forgiveness. In giving there are mutual benefits, both to the giver and the receiver. There is infinite love and freedom as we give of ourselves and what we have with others. In the end, love is an action word. Throughout these exercises, we have moved from thoughts of love to learning to truly express love for one another. To truly love people, we need to take action on that love. That action is giving.

6) *The Power of Self-Love*

I encourage you to embrace self-love. I know, I know, we hear this all the time! Move beyond the "head knowledge" to bring it into your very being. You can begin by embracing the love that comes from other people around you. As you holistically drink in love from others, it will begin to permeate your feelings, your thoughts, your beliefs. Your awareness of love for yourself will emerge. Love yourself and let people love you. Recognize that you have the right to say no and sometimes, you have the need to say yes. If you are presented with a decision or an opportunity that does not align with your inner knowing, that source of power within you, say no. Saying NO will actually make your YES more powerful and appreciated. So many times we are saying yes to so many things that we become overwhelmed and overburdened. Say yes to those things that align with your purpose, self-love, and align with Joy Consciousness.

Most of all take care of you! Not taking care of yourself, not feeding good things into your body, mind, and spirit will cause you to visit dis-ease consciousness more frequently. Take care of your temple. It is very difficult to live in a state of joy when you are not eating the right foods, getting proper rest and exercising your body. Right now, I give you permission to live a life full of joy, passion, and happiness. It's your right, and it's right there for you. Embrace and love yourself.

No one is immune to the stuff of life. Life is full of joys and pleasure, bangs and bruises, unexpected grief and breathtaking sunsets. It is all life!

Embracing joy, tapping into our power source, enacting the power of forgiveness, and loving full out does not protect us from difficulties and challenges. What it gives us is usable, dependable, and reliable tools to step out of the personal identification we create with life's pain points. Stuff happens! It is what we choose to do with the stuff that sets us up for victory and longer lasting Joy.

I encourage you to read these pages more than once and embrace these thoughts of encouragement. Set yourself up for success with these habits: guard the people you share your time with, seek counsel only of those that are where you want to be in your life, and from those people, reach out and ask for help. Then, move forward and return the gift to those that need you.

Be mindful of all the things you take in.

- Food – Eat healthful foods that feed your being. Make your calories count! Celebrate your temple with whole food rich in nutrients. When you do so, you'll find that there is no room for empty calories.

- Music, movies, reading – Many of us don't realize all the empty minutes that we lose with what we watch, read and listen to. Even more seriously, watching violence and negativity is like eating seriously unhealthy foods. We take in all that we watch, read and listen to. The news is probably the worst source of negative energy of all! Consider going on a news and TV fast. Fill that time with a new hobby. Play games with friends and family, take a long walk or have a good, deep conversation. Celebrate your temple! Always ask the question, how does this activity serve me? Is this working for me or against me? Is this pushing me in a state of Joy Consciousness or Dis-ease? You will be surprised at how much time you actively choose to place yourself in a state of Dis-ease.

CONCLUSION

Know that where you are right now at this moment, you are a perfect, wondrous, beautiful being. You are enough right now. You deserve all love. Each one of us is here to experience great joy, great pleasure, great love, great peace, and great beauty. Lasting joy is possible. You just have to believe it is possible for you!

The six stages you've read here, when consistently applied, will develop new patterns, and new ways of thinking and believing. Start today and take the first step to tap into your Power Source. Each day you do so, will be a little better than the last--even on your most challenging days.

Won't you join me on this journey to Joy Consciousness? I pray you'll allow God to bring clarity and give you answers, just as he did for me. He has your back! His desire is for you to be victorious! You have your own Power Source just waiting for you to tap into it.

I love you,

Monica

WITH GRATITUDE

First and foremost, I would like to thank my significant other and close friend, Rod Brown for standing beside me throughout the transition in my career and writing this book. You taught me what real love is, inspired me to improve my knowledge, and move forward in my purpose. You are my source of solace, and I dedicate this book to you.

I would also thank my wonderful daughter, Micah, for always making me smile. You taught me how to reach higher levels of Joy Consciousness. I hope that one day you can read this book and truly understand the depths of which you are loved.

I'd like to thank my parents and grandparents for allowing me to struggle in my childhood. A great deal of stretching came from the struggle and without it, I would not be the woman that I am now. Although there was struggle, I know that you all love me with everything you have in you. I see that now more than ever...I love you and honor you all.

I want to thank my siblings. Although we are an interestingly blended family, you all have chosen to embrace love. Every time I am in your presence, gratitude fills my heart because I know that our relationship is nothing short of a miracle. It is a constant reminder that with love and forgiveness, all things are possible.

I would like to thank my close friends who support me, lift me up but have always kept me grounded in grace throughout this journey, and most of all made me laugh! I can pick up the phone at any time and know, without a doubt, that by the end of the call my spirit will be lifted. A dose of medicine that I take with pleasure.

Last, but certainly not least, with everything in me, I want to thank God for loving me enough to open his arms and cover me with His grace. For showing me that life is supposed to be filled with love, abundance and most of all JOY!

ABOUT MONICA

Monica Lewis is an entrepreneur, author and Power Alignment Coach. In 2006, Monica co-founded, The Solace Group, a consulting firm dedicated to helping Mental Health organizations in the areas of expansion, operations and programming. The Solace Group grew to become a beacon of leadership in the Mental Health Industry, consulting with hundreds of organizations all over the country. In 2010, The Solace Group decided to put the theory to practice to co-launch a brick and mortar Mental Health Clinic. Five years later, Monica and her partners sold the clinic for seven figures - an extremely rare feat in the Mental Health industry.

Monica is now the CEO and founder of Source Thought and the Coaching Development Director for Not Just Weight. Source Thought is a motivational and inspirational company that provides personal development, business coaching and products dedicated to spiritual growth and lifelong learning. Not Just Weight is a wellness program that combines the principles of Naturopathic Medicine, Lifestyle Medicine and Mindset to promote an easy transition into a healthier life.

Monica overcame an impoverished and unstable childhood with a drug abusing parent to owning and consulting for million dollar organizations. Her escape from a tumultuous past to business and personal success is what drives her desires to teach others to become their own change agents. Monica's overall mission, no matter the platform, is helping people see the grandest vision of themselves, then holding them accountable to realize it.

To learn more about Monica visit, www.iamsourcethought.com or www.notjustweight.com.